Lionhearted;
Poetry and spoken word collection

Aiméè Keenan

chipmunkapublishing
the mental health publisher

Aiméè Keenan

All rights reserved, no part of this publication may be reproduced by any means, electronic, mechanical photocopying, documentary, film or in any other format without prior written permission of the publisher.

>   Published by
>   Chipmunkapublishing
>   United Kingdom

http://www.chipmunkapublishing.com

Copyright © Aiméè Keenan 2019

Cover photography @ Amanda Ekström

An aria of awakening

We fail to see what's real and beautiful when we are asleep.

"Closed eyes, She walked, blinded, oblivious to earth's sweet surprises. Moments dragged and people passed — noisy, unkind and dark.
Hopeful, she fought her way through the bushes, catching growing glimpses of luminous light; sensing the sweet scent of love's light and jubilant joys.
Breaking down the wall of fear's fierce force,
Out into the silent sea she stepped,
Never looking back to the poisonous pangs of past's painful persistence.
Into the new mysterious maze of aromatic arias and blissful beauty,
she opened her eyes to the endless aether, awakened, at last, to the freedom of life's fruitful forest, the power of present's path and those wondrous eyes of endless ecstasy."

❤**Life can surprise you. Joy is often hidden beneath the clouds that try to drown you in pain** ❤

Aiméè Keenan

Naïve normality

"Be normal", they said.
"Why read that" they questioned? "That's so weird", they laughed. All the while she laughed silently to herself, dreaming dangerously of skies of blue and plains of green, of ravishing red roses and luscious lilies, of ecstatic evenings and proud performances. She danced daintily, alone, but not lonely, spinning splendidly in sentimental circles under the encapsulating essence of August's majestic, momentous moonlight. In ignorance of their caged minds, under the serene stars she swam softly in the early morning seamless sea, as sensuous sentiments flowed fearlessly through her wandering, melodious mind. Through painful perseverance she persisted, opening inch by inch, the gates to the freedom that lay before her.

♥Make every day count. Fill it doing what you love, living the purpose you came here for, the one you dream of. Go skinny dipping under the stars. Roll around. Be a kid. Take risks. Good risks. Stop caring what everyone else thinks. **WHAT OTHERS THINK OF YOU IS NONE OF YOUR BUSINESS, SO MIND IT!**♥

The cheerful child

Still sleeping,
She danced freely in liberating lengths along the dance floor. Ignoring imperfections, she circled carelessly, unafraid of the jurisdictional judgments of the party, for she in blooming freedom, cared not for the harshness of their limited lights.
Stare; they did— for crazy she did seem in her bliss, arms jumping joyfully as she jolted joyously to the melodious music.
Sober amidst the alcoholic aroma,
her star seeking soul sparked ethereal energy and twinkled in the chaotic calmness of the crowd.
And there he danced too, crazy and carefree and he caught her eye.
Unawakened and unaware, she did not see him in his full splendour, but sure she did *see* him, noticing his joyful spirit through her wandering eyes.
"Oh how wonderful", she pondered, watching him carefully as he bounced in bliss; until the cruelty of evil's ego stole her soul away from his recognition,
for young they were and much journey left to learn before they'd meet again.

Aiméè Keenan

♥Do not give up who you are to fit in with the crowd. Be you and it won't be long 'til you will be leading your own crowd. We do not always see things clearly at first; forgive it. When you awaken it will fill you with joy to see what you hadn't seen before ♥

Don't you get it?

Don't you get it?
You matter. A lot! A damn lot!
You matter so much it's unbelievable how much you matter.
I want to belt it to the world at the top of my voice and shatter it through every pane of glass until it explodes into the world sending little fragments of faith throughout the entire world. I want to sing it at the highest frequencies 'till it pinches your ears and throw your sparkling dust into the universe in an aromatic array of sunshine.
I want to roar it from the rooftops and scream it in sirens throughout every city, awakening you all one by one, little by little, until you bloody get it – 'til you bloody get it!!!!!
You're enough!!! God dammit!!! YOU. ARE. ENOUGH!!!!
Why don't you get it?
YOU STILL DON'T GET IT?
You've been told SO MANY TIMES.

Why don't you believe them?
They tell you all the time!
And you're still choosing to stay in that fear?

It's not you, sweet child, it's not you.

Aiméè Keenan

Why are you hiding from yourself?
Burying yourself in the mud and pulling yourself away from the light?
--Hiding from the REAL YOU.
Do you think they really give a hoot who you are?
No! So why bother contemplating their opinions, their unrequited, odourless opinions.
I thought you didn't care what they thought of you?
I thought you weren't afraid?
I thought if, you were – somehow afraid, as every human is, you'd trust enough by now to smash through fear's fierce wall and step out in perfect harmony into your tasteful triumph, winning wondrously with every fibre in your sparkling soul?

You preach it, but you can't face it.

You tell them they are breaking free.

You say… "Feel the fear and do it anyway".

You tell them that if they want it enough, they will find a way to make it happen, if it means enough. But you don't. No. YOU don't. Not when it matters. Not with what's REAL.

Lionhearted

You encourage their energetic epiphanies and social sways, and praise their purposeful paragraphs and weird ways…
Yet you remain untrue to your teachings in a saddened part of you; In the TRUEST part of you!
There you are, retreating into a ball on the floor,
Ridden by social conventions and caged like a bird in it's dark, devious corner, starved of its nourishing nutrition and trapped in its tortuous tent; you've forgotten how to fly.
Your wings…they've…shrunk.

Well enough. ENOUGH is ENOUGH!!!!!
The time has come to eradicate the pangs of your insecurities,
To face your lack of deep self-love,
Of destructive self- comparison;
To face the fear of your beautiful, attractive innocence and finally encapsulate yourself in the pending power of surrounding, luminous love that awaits you.

It's time.
…Time to get washed away in love's beauty and drown yourself in dangerous, magical moments of earth's glorious gift - LOVE.
A gift which until now, you would not even GIVE TO YOURSELF.

So take it.
Face it.
Breathe it. Just breathe. Breathe.
Every piece of you, you think imperfect, is invigorating. Ever scar…it's so sweet.
Every word, is wonderful;
Every smile….sensational.
Every part of you exudes bountiful beauty; inside and out.
Every laugh…oh...it's so lovely.
Every inch of your intelligence is inviting and every speck of your spirit is sacred.

You are enough.
You are MORE than enough.

You're bloody brilliant.

--------Have you heard me yet?

♥**You are enough, you are so enough, it's unbelievable how enough you are. This is something you must understand, in the darkest of times. YOU MATTER.**♥

Demeanour

His face, beautiful and enlightened in all his childhood innocence,
Lit countless dark nights in her sweet heart;
For his daring demeanour and frivolous freedom
She knew must play a part,
In the journey of her mystical chart.

♥**Kindness is a quality that should not be overlooked. Open your eyes to see the beauty, the mystery, the fun, the joy. But most of all, trust yourself and believe in the extraordinary.**♥

Aiméè Keenan

Eyes of innocence

Your eyes, wondrously wide and
Intriguingly interesting, melt my heart and
speak sonnets to my sparkling soul.
One look,
The world around me
fades into an aromatic abyss
of heavenly hope for the days ahead,
dreams of evenings encapsulated in ecstasy,
and a future filled with child-like captivation as
our magical melody is played.

♥Listen. See. Hear. Feel. Touch. Stop spending too much time thinking. Focus on what's real - Nature - Senses- Life - Love.♥

Gripped

The repetition; choking, gripping,
Driving the light from their eyes, pulling the strings of persistent patience;
Heads held in hands, maddened, bored and insignificant.
Pointlessness, mundaneness; empty words delivered on an empty line;
Zombies crawling in discomfort and dislike, trembling in the harsh reality of piercing purposelessness.
Mannequin audio robots, drifting; fine-tuned by the wasted words,
All for the good but losing their cause;
Losing their minds,
Gritting their teeth,
Shaking their heads,
Supressing their anger,
Crumbling in boredom;
The madness -
Crazy;
Crazy in the normality of their ground hog lives;
Life lived for the hour,
Every minute lost, buried treasure and lost forever –
Absorbed, trapped, painful and disgusting.
A life stolen by time, stolen by birth,

Aiméè Keenan

Carved by circumstance and wrapped with worry.
Swimming to the surface: no time for air,
No time to breathe;
Falling in the common call –
The only way apparent to sleeping eyes.
A way of hoping, dreaming; imagining all the while a life less lonesome than the lonely calls;
One more victorious than that of systematic sounds.
If only that light could be lit,
That song could be sung.
For freedom is the only true hope;
Freedom – a lost ingredient of the ancient book of spells;
The hidden treasure on the pirate's search,
A lost ingredient of the tasteful recipe; ripped out, banished, forbidden, stolen away by the wicked wizard.
He; weak in his power, evil in his ecstasy
Pulling their hearts ferociously from their chests,
Squeezing them, testing them, tempting them.
But one day they'll claim their long lost gift and stolen treasure,
Cut off the reigns of their forceful entrapment,
And sail the silent seas in rightful freedom and imperfect peace,
As they float in bliss, treading gently upon the waves of wonder and limitless love: purpose.

Lionhearted

♥Stop giving in to the monotonous life. You weren't made to be a robot - so be a human being. Do what calls you and stop expecting yourself to be happy fitting into the system.♥

Aiméè Keenan

Rainbow skies

When love's lost symphony sings,
And melody's magic cries,
I dream of angel's wings
Where heart's true splendour lies

In the distant hills I hear
The calling of your soul
Though true loves path is clear
Your mind still takes its toll

Though envious eyes can see
The fears of distant sighs,
I know your soul is free
O'er rainbow skies it flies

One day those scars will peel,
Your heart's true lights will shine
Fine feelings will reveal true love –
'Till then, others; I'll decline.

♥**You only get one heart. Love it**♥

Perfect parallels

The perfect picture, envisioned in the movie of my momentous mind,
As the film roll reveals a thousand scenes of a thousand ways I'd tell you how my heart dances to the sound of your sweet song.
Revealed in unexpected urgency,
arising my ecstatic excitement at the learning of your loves return,
I wait in aromatic anticipation of the meeting of our eyes;
Until suddenly and all at once,
my treasurable tower comes crashing down in broken parts strewn over the tear stricken floor. Falling from endless expectation into prudent painful puddles,
my tears speak of shattered songs and martyred melodies.
Rejected ripples roll along the river of my heart's weary blood,
shedding silently as my tempered tastes tear away at my mind's melancholic music.
Under the pale moonlight;
 My dreams drift drearily, wrapping themselves wondrously, wishing,
waiting, saving themselves for another time,
Another day,
Another moment,
For another spark —

When our vibrant vibrations meet in perfect positions …in perfect parallels.

♥Beauty surrounds you. Never forget that. Not for one moment. There is always light. ALWAYS love. Even those at the brink of tragedy can often see it - so let yourself be one who sees.♥

Glittering Grace

There you are — You've got me once again–
Enthralled by your energetic surprises,
Your gorgeous gifts
And colourful creativity;
Amazing me with your wonderful ways
And your seamless senses.
Here I lie — hopelessly hooked on your
captivating chords and heavenly harmonies,
as the sound of your golden melodies emanate
energetically while your fingers float blissfully
over the orient keys.
O how your gentle disposition and tender
tastes liberate my thickening shield,
And with each nostalgic note,
my mind floats off to far off lands where
immortal love listens to the chaotic calls of our
warbling wishes - wrapping them up in
blissful blankets of sunset's mirage and
glittering them in glorious godly grace.

♥**To awaken is to see. To appreciate is the greatest power. And when you see, you cannot "unsee".**♥

Aiméè Keenan

A million wondrous ways

Dreaming of delightful days,
Hoping for happy holidays and peaceful
parties;
Knowing how it feels to love you;
Imagining a million wondrous ways in which
our stars would meet magically for the first
truthful time, where we entwine our fingers in
epiphanic essays,
Surrendering to our souls sweet song
And floating fearlessly on a bed of cosy clouds
that carry us on our purposeful paths.
Sprinkling little flakes of faith and fortune over
fields afar,
and lighting lakes of magical melancholy,
we ignite the ravaging romantic rhythms of
our harmonious hearts and glitter graciously
through the golden gates of glorious, fearless
freedom.

♥Flow with the formless, dream, imagine. Your imagination is a gift, often stolen at our approach to adolescence. Grip it as tight as you can, never letting go. ♥

Hidden treasure

Isolated, alone, yet in sweet companionship
She made her way through the silver snow,
Each foot leaving crisp crunches
As she pondered peacefully under the soft moonlight.
The moon threw a beautiful ray of glimmering light
Over the blissful bed of white,
Casting her sensuous spell over the mountainous land as winter cradled cautiously it's wondrous creation
With all its freezing warmth.
Silent and still, the stars twinkled truthfully,
Telling sensational stories to the moon
Who smiled back softly to her faithful friends
In beautiful beams of love and joy,
Sprinkling upon them through her eager eyes,
this heartful gift on this sweet silent night.
Suddenly, the glimmering girl stopped in her tracks, frozen by the sheer boundless beauty
of the sight that lay before her.
She gazed gleefully at earth's innocence
Of deliberate careful creation; such a heavenly house appeared- a palace; a paradise, it would seem, to those who choose to see it so.
And see, she did, with every spark in her soul -
She felt it in her bones, no longer alone.
She heard it in the distance; buzzing, chiming,

Aiméè Keenan

Twinkling in turbulent tranquillity;
For the universe danced in all her
Glorious glamour, leaving a secret
Trail of humble gifts for the children, the
awakened, the seeing; the kind.

♥ **Don't forget about the birds, the butterflies, all the beautiful creatures. You may think you are too busy to notice them. Don't underestimate the power and magic of something so small.** ♥

Beauty in truth

Beauty's all around, beauty is within.
In the battles we lose, and the battles we win.
Beauty's not just what the eye can perceive,
but rather an image of what we believe.
Love is the feeling that lives in our heart
though sometimes it struggles to play out its part.
Love is not fearful nor anger nor pain, it's the comforting blanket that we must regain.
 So if you are worried, or anxious or sad, just look deep inside, you have all that you need.

♥**There is love hidden in every crevice, every corner, every tunnel, every pit. Whether or not you see it depends on whether or not you choose to believe it.**♥

Nature's tranquillity; human tranquillity

The gleaming sun dances vibrant rays over the snowy hills,
Lighting the icy pathways as they glitter magnificently in their boundless beauty,
warming the freezing air in perfect patterns of fresh heat and tasteful tranquillity.
The mountains rise marvellously into the singing skies of blue,
Protecting the land peacefully with their perfect presence and hugging heights; lit lovingly by the sun in all its sweet sensations.
For the hills were made for dancing, the hills were made for loving;
and what is not to love in this unending epiphany of the universe: with its secret surprises and helpful hands for the one who dares to ask.
Hidden amongst the hollows of the hills, sweet soliloquys send mysterious messages to the leaning listener;
as life's treasure twirls in twinkling circles, waiting wisely to be swept up by some silent searcher, who longs lovingly to share his gift with the worried world and lighten a hurting heart or two into perfect peace and swaying balance;

until all the world falls unconditionally in love with no regret,
no pain, no bitterness, no fury, no sadness.

♥The Universe is flashing it's magic right in front of your eyes, waving it right in front of your face, screaming it in your ears. Magic is powerful. But it's also precious. Therefore you will only see it if you believe it - so it's best to start believing!♥

Aiméè Keenan

Light in love's darkness

She dreamed of him in the night
Trusting her inspired intuition,
Always believing her heart may be right,
To fall straight back to the turbulent fight.

She danced through the singing street,
She sang with the birds as they glittered past .
Dreaming of laughter and nights O so sweet
Feeling that soon their sweet hearts would
sure meet.

But ecstatic smiles did end,
For dancing dreams do not always appear,
Her mind had a gift at playing pretend,
And into the night sad hopes it did send.

And here as she fell
She sang louder that day,
For perfect rejection gave freedom in rays;
Dreams and fortunes not always aligned,
But hope for the future flew higher those days.

♥**Trust yourself. Trust in the flow. Do not expect yourself to get everything right all of the time. There's ALWAYS a silver lining to every dark cloud. Light comes from pain…it just depends on how you look at things.**♥

Lionhearted

Run through the thorns with the heart of a lion,
Ride through the waves on a stormy day,
Smile through the pain as it pulls you down,
Reach for the stars though the people frown.

Life's like a river with rocks on the way,
Take them in hand and build an empire,
Dive in the deep end if they tell you no,
It'll take you to places of glorious flow.

Stop sitting, stop searching, just step up and start,
Stop looking for someone to hand you the part,
For dreams do not chase you, or choose you or wait,
They are yours if you conquer with courage at heart.

❤**Spread your wings. You were born to fly. Roar your message like a lion. You were born to speak your word**❤

Aiméè Keenan

Look away, look away

What are these horrid thoughts
That creep up in me in the day,
Taking over me;
Throwing me back towards the ground;
Underwater; into the deep end – into the danger zone.
The devil in my mind shouts softly in my ear
words of disillusionment, fear and self-punishment;
And so I wallow in my own pathetic pity
Of my lost hurting heart and shattered soul.
I'm falling, drowning;
Wishing the towering mountains would suddenly open up,
Swallow me and cradle me in their warm embrace,
Hide me from the dying world ,
Give me the love that's lost;
Isolate me from the hate,
From the fearful world;
Where love is buried
Feet deep beneath the
Freezing winter snow,
Unaffected by the sun's smile as it spreads its wings o'er the woolly blanket:
powerless in its painful attempts to heat the purposeless plains;

Lionhearted

Leaving icicles hanging where flowers should bloom,
And silence where birds should sing.
I'm lost:
Lost in the emptiness inside;
Fallen in the void of minus ten,
Crying out for help,
Begging, crawling, shaking.
But they can't see
For they are blinded by their own self
Obsession and meaningless motives;
Leaving me there to contemplate my own self-destructive hatred and pitiful pain; trapped.
Temporarily.
Until I SEE.
Until I pull myself out of this bottomless pit of nothingness.
Until I crawl, limb by limb,
Inch by inch,
To the crack in the frozen ice wall
That captivates my shivering body;
Stepping through the gifted gap,
Into the heat, the light, the sun;
A second chance.

♥ **I KNOW there will be days every bone in your body is filled with darkness and you can never imagine stepping past it. But you CAN. And you will. When you start to think about giving up,**

Aiméè Keenan

remember it doesn't matter how many times you fall but how many times you get back up on your feet even if the dark is heavier than anything you have ever felt.♥

Smile for the saddened

Love: embedded in their hearts,
We let in the light once again
And fill their minds with just a glimmer of hope,
A happy thought, a thought of freedom.
And little did you know, your simple touch,
One sweet smile, could change a world;
Change the universe of a saddened soul
To one of vibrant lights,
Where bright colours rise like fireworks
In the near distance, shooting sparks of
Freedom, peace and love in their newly
Blooming world of friendly faces and
Speculating opportunity; of freedom and
fantasy; of ecstasy, of compassion –
Unconditional love.

❤ **When you start to feel sorry for yourself, remember there is someone out there who feels the same, or who is in a much worse position than you . A SIMPLE SMILE could change a life. That may seem impossible, but every single action has an impact. MAKE YOUR IMPACT COUNT. A truthful smile can translate into the most beautiful words.** ❤

Aiméè Keenan

A tale of heart and mind

"Life is love" ; I uttered.
If so; "then what is love?" I questioned.
Hard and long I thought to find the perfect
answer to this querulous question,
Yet nothing made my heart sing so beautifully
as to the calling of your soul to mine.
 "He is love", my heart responded.
"Don't be pathetic", said my meticulous mind,
 "He is not love. For he cannot love you. Who
are you to think such pretty thoughts?".
"Who am I not to think such admirable
thoughts?" replied the heart,
"why must you seek to cut through my
delicate flowering walls with your bloody
knife, destroying the blooming buds of the
graceful joy that waltzes in my veins?"
"Your frustrations I do not understand my
dear heart," cried the mind,
"for I seek merely to protect you from the
fantasies of your true desires, keeping you
from the creation of your idyllic illusions, for
you cannot choose the life you want. You must
remain confined in the teachings of your
world, your school, your home, your system;
you must have only the things this home may
give you: nothing more. For you are not as
great as those you dance for. This is your
belonging; your destiny and only those who
wish to face true fear may conquer this

confinement; and you, my sweet, do not hold such strength."

The hopeful heart in soft symphonic song replied, "Think what you wish dear mind; I thank you. For you have given me more than I could have asked - the perfect answer indeed. For in your lack of belief, you inspire me; I cannot please everyone; your limits cannot define me. Now I seek nothing but freedom beyond the bars of this confinement into which you entrap me."
Smiling joyfully to herself, the beaming heart bounced gleefully on her way, knocking on my welcoming doors;
 filling every space with new and glistening air: air of knowing; filling every crevice of my being with luminous loving light;
 "Uncertainty no more" laughed the heart, "For no moaning of no mischievous mind will ruin the remnants of my dancing dreams."

Stupefied, the bewildered mind fell back in pangs of awe at hearts true strength; "Dear heart, you have passed. You've overcome the testing and trials of my darkness, now we must work together. For you have proved that I alone do not know. I am not true knowledge; this is you. I am not strength; this is you. I am not guidance, for you have skipped along another path but mine. I am not love; for I failed to love. You are all these things; but alone, you will not shield

yourself, feed yourself, see the physicality and the troubles of our world. But if we work together, we shall know all, love all, trust and see. Can you forgive me, heart?"
"For I am love and cannot refused to forgive such an amorous plea. Yes, together we shall grow for we shall have eyes to see, ears to hear and love to feel," sang the heart.
And so together they climbed the mountain. Together they reached the top; unmarked, untouched, unscathed, complete.
"Life is love" I uttered once again,
"With a heart to find and mind to reason, with these gifts no peak is unobtainable; for life is love and I have all I seek already in inside this posing corpse; wrapped, waiting, glowing.

♥ Don't let your mind take over, when your heart is telling you what you truly know. You would not survive without your heart. Nor your mind. Work with them both, let them be friends. Calm your mind, let it lead you, but listen to your heart. It has ALL of the answers to every one of your questions. ♥

Love's forgotten truth

Tell me, tell me….
What's it all for?
The rushing, the panic, the crazy?
The fights, the sadness, the anxiety,
All for one day;
One day whose meaning has been stripped away,
Forgotten, buried amongst the towers of
Tedious toys and mountains of mess,
Shop floors ridden with undesired items
Flung in fury and frustration,
Streets packed with cars, incautious, unkind,
People pushing persistently to arrive at their destination,
Eyes closed, unseeing of the happenings in their eyes,
As the others sit wrapped in broken blankets on the street sides,
Turbulent yet content in acceptance of their terrible fates,
Unaware of the burning spark still dancing in their hearts,
The buried dreams, dangerously entrapped in the weeds
Of their windy worries and hurtful hatred; Lost in the twisted pathways of their sunken minds.
One smile is all they ask.
On look of love.

Aiméè Keenan

One thought, one glance, one little acknowledgement.
And you don't even give such a simple gift.
A simple gift.
Penniless.
Free.
Yet beautiful.
A gift so small, yet so powerful,
A seed so simple, that can save a life, unwind the weeds and unfasten the knives, unravelling soul's true beauty – love.

♥ **Don't get caught up in the materials; in all of the 'things ' in life. Yes, they are important – appreciate them. But never lose sight of the true meaning of it all. Be present, be kind, and the world will be kind to you.** Care for the unfortunate.♥

The wasted waiting woman

There she cradled herself in the corner of her saddened street,
waiting hopelessly at his dying door,
gift glowing in her hand,
growing greater each day in its depth,
expanding as each day went by.
She swayed, dreaming of him, picturing,
imagining the day he'd finally accept her gift.
She smiled through the days and danced through the nights ,
for the hope in her heart held tightly to her loving gift,
in full refusal to retire from it's painful persistence.
Yet people passed, days passed, moment moved.
The sun rose; the sun fell; stars twinkled, stars disappeared.
The moon warned her of the movie passing before her blinded eyes; for she would not move herself one inch from that dreamy door.
Love passed, dancing before her eyes,
Tapping her shoulder,
Touching her breaking heart with all its force:
Yet asleep she remained.
Asleep in the spell upon her heart, asleep and unawakened to the paths passing before her.
For in joyful waiting she became blind,
oblivious and trapped.

Trapped in an ignorant illusion; blind to the endless opportunities rolling right before her burning eyes.
Until she woke at the end of clock's time, and for a split second, before the breaking of her glass; did realise the sleep that she'd been in.
"Too late," said the moon.
For the show is over and you failed to play the part, now you must accept the loss your of blind attachment"
She slipped away into the dimming night, saddened, empty, disappointed, wasted.

❤ **If you spend your life waiting, life will pass you by. Don't miss the opportunities, focus on the past; on the broken. Live for NOW. It will bring you much more joy when you master it. TAKE ACTION towards your dreams. Everything is there in place for you. But friends, you've got to grab what is yours, before it's too late. Who cares if they say you can't. I'm telling you now…YOU CAN.**❤

Hypnotic entrapment

I see you there, floating,
Shining bright with light bursting at the seams. Hidden in the stream of subtle safety she entraps you with her cold warmth, her fake generosity, sweeping you up
In secret slavery,
Loving you with her selfish sorcery,
Hypnotising you with her humorous, heavy heart and manipulative mind.
Yet you do not see.
And there they watch carefully by the side,
One by one witnessing the silence of your words and
Limits of your fluttering freedom as you
 Dwell in the inescapable nest of her artistic advantage.
They scream, they shout, they shake you, But under gentle hypnotic hands, asleep you stay, for no power, no true love, no hearts confession could even wake you from the trance of your silent sleep walk.
 Until one day in a magical miracle,
I'd take you gently by the hand, awakening your drifting mind, and filling every ounce of your spirit with ecstatic epiphany. You smile once more, within; not just without; forevermore.

Aiméè Keenan

♥ You might have been asleep for a long time, but I promise one day you will awaken. And when you do, you will see colours you've never seen before. Sometimes we become trapped in the dreams of others, in the desires of others, denying our own hopes, dreams and visions. YOU are the one who writes your story. Make it a FAIRYTALE and not a horror story. ♥

Healing of the shattered soul

Here I am on the other side,
Light shed upon the quarrels of my heart,
Flowing peacefully at last in knowing;
Knowing of the gorgeous gift and miraculous magic of that prolific power.
Tears strewn o'er my grief stricken face,
As virtuous visions of my fractured future
Fall in horrific harmony on the tortured tiles,
I smile at last in heavy happiness as freedom flies elegantly through worry's window,
calmly collecting in all its glittering glory,
every ounce of my shattered spirit;
healing it, entwining it in love, putting back the pieces in perfect pictures, pulling me out, fixing me, loving me in heaven's harmony, rocking me gently in heartful hands, until in careful courage I step up once again,
Foot by foot,
Day by day
Month by month; Aligned.

❤ **Have faith. Have hope. Hope is what brings us out of the darkness even when we cannot see a thing. There is always hope, always light, always something to be grateful for. We just have to choose between giving up and having COURAGE.**❤

Aiméè Keenan

Unrequited abandonment

Stepping into darkness, I dwell pensively, savouring the sweet sensations of your intimate interactions.
Jolting feverishly in flavorous fury,
I dive fearfully into the unknown abyss of sweet sadness and endless longing for soul's careful company; trembling, despairing, shivering.
Knowing of your unrequited urgency and charming desire for jubilant domination,
I reside in hope beneath the suspicious stars for their flickering fate to throw a tasteful turbulent turn upon the position of our saddened situation.
I stop; I stare; hopeless; glancing dreamily at the moon as she stretches her heavy hand towards my fading face,
placing purposefully in my fingertips a letter of her losing love as she pushes purposefully my tender silver spirit with every ounce of selfless dormant disinterest.
There I lie, empty; yet full, pensive; yet silent, awake; though sleeping; free; though jailed, wounded; yet wondrous.

♥ **There's no light without dark. It's Ying and Yang. There's always a reason behind everything, but it's all about perspective. It's okay to be sad, to feel down, to cry. Let it out. Be patient and accept.**

Lionhearted

But most of all, let yourself be healed – be kind to your heart. You must firstly learn to refill your own cup, before you can serve others.♥

Aiméè Keenan

The fruit of her creation

There she stood in all her splendour;
Gleaming and glistening; radiating in rapid
rays her humble heart's love,
besotted beautifully like a mother over her
new born child as she cradles the fruit of her
caring creation in her heated hands.
Proud, jubilant and overwhelmed by spirits
illimitable harmony,
She soars in perfect purpose;
gathering with her touching spirit and helpful
hands; many souls in beautiful bliss', in
wonder, in ecstatic experience.
For a moment she looks on, watching;
Eyes tearful in her effulgent gratitude.

❤ **When a soul begins to live it's purpose, it starts to GLOW, and nothing can stop this. It's the most beautiful thing to witness. Ever look at someone and see their eyes radiating, and they just emanate so much joy it almost knocks you off your feet? Nothing more powerful than a purpose being lived, and lived to the full. It's infectious; and some people are just born to inspire. You may be one.** ❤

Words

Words cannot describe you, my love.
For you are more than words,
More than poems, more than rhyme,
More than every beautiful glimpse of carefully
crafted calligraphy upon a perfect page.
You are the essence; my beyond.
You are my glimpse of all; my dreams.
You're my thoughts; my magic memories.
My future, my present, my every moment.
You are happiness – you are my dance;
My sweet song.
You are tears, yet my smile.
You're the fear, drowned in hope.
You're the anger, yet - you ARE the light.
But most of all, glittering joy,
You are my love; my greatest love;
For you ARE love.

♥ **Do you think we will ever find the words to describe a force so powerful? Well, I don't, because it is beyond words. The energy of the universe – it's so mysterious and you are part of it…so don't ever let words bring you down, because YOU, are also beyond anything that words could describe.**♥

Aiméè Keenan

BOXED

What is life?
Some sort of dream, some illusion, in which
we control the outcome by the throw of our
own die?
Do we choose the number on which it lands,
or is it a pre- planned game of ready written
cheats that we must learn to follow?
Robots walking through the crowded streets,
boxed up, box after box, telephone in hand -
one box; retreating to our box homes to watch
our box televisions - another box, living our
boxed lives with boxed up love....
We're boxed in a box, inside a box and buried
inside another huge box.
We go to work....
We walk through the boxed up system in
which we human beings are entrapped;
without purpose; passionless.
We walk in circles 'til we hit a brick wall,
bouncing back brutally as we land on the
splintering floor.
Arising we see the mountain unravel itself
once again before our eyes: another hill to
climb, another game to grow, another pain to
persist.
 Yet then, awakening, they think they've
broken free to dance through life - money no

longer a worry, holding on to their endless physical possessions and worldly gains, their petty achievements and epiphanic triumphs; all for the satisfaction of the egoic mind, yet they believe not to be ego -
What for, they ask?
"I've got everything I ever wished for but the emptiness remains."
For what is the purpose of it all?
Why the pain?
Why the pleasure?
Why do what we do?
To please others?
To look good ?
To fit in?
To look amazing on our boxed up Facebook page?
For a sense of achievement?
For WHAT???!!!
Why bother?
Who are we trying to please?
Life is a dream people -
It's merely an illusion .
You are not you;
For you cannot be what you are also watching.
Rather, we are the spectators of a true life within;
A life more than physical, more than achievement, more than artefacts:
A life that is indestructible,

Transformational, ever changing, ever knowing.
A life that is love.
For it IS love...
And we are love.
It is the only 'THING';
The energy from which all life stems;
A powerful creation.
People say THEY create?
I say LOVE creates.
The greater the love; the more the creation -
For love IS the creator And we ARE love.
Love is the source; the force behind every action; good and bad.
Some choose to let it in
To surrender to it, release;
And doing so let in the boundless creation that true love's source brings.
So what is our purpose they ask?
Our purpose, I say, is to be happy; to find things that make you happy.
People who make happy.
And how does one be happy they ask?
Happiness is to love unconditionally,
In allowance;
In surrendering to the ever changing rules of life's game.
For we do not know where we are heading, we do not know when our light of love shall transform out of this physical existence.
We do not know the past,

Lionhearted

The future,
Nor the end .
So our purpose is to let love in, to see it in everyone:
To flow with love -
To live the unexpected path of our blinded mind, to see the beauty in front of you, before it's gone.
For it will make you breathe,
It will grow your heart
And grow your life in starry ways and unimagined instances.
So yes, love's children
Your purpose,
As they ask,

Is to love... And be loved.

♥**Think outside of the box and look in from the outside. Put the phone down, breathe the fresh air. Learn to just be. It's a powerful feeling. Your purpose is to love.**♥

Aiméè Keenan

Tearing through years

There you stand in your bitterness,
Dropping silent tears from years of pain,
Crawling feverishly in the hurtful shame,
Abandoning loved ones for past's poor performance,
Rolling religiously in moments gone and memories made;
Memories of pity, of fear of anger.
There you wallow in the pit of anger's valley,
Encapsulating yourself in anger's abundance
And hatred's horrid hands.
All for what?
All for the sad satisfaction of your unempathetic ego,
Turning your head from the dear ones
To fill the satisfaction of your trapped mind;
A mind trapped in ignorant images and fleeting fury;
Letting slip of the beauty you once held in your
Hopeful heart; all for the sake of silly spite
And unresolved occurrences.
Blind you are in this moment of danger;
Blind to the blooming flowers of your own Mothers' womb,
Closing your eyes from her light,
The life before your heavy heart;
The fruit of your own relative;

Lionhearted

The unbreakable bond written in the silent
pages of your heart. So open them, love's child,
before death's duty removes these gifted
human bonds and leaves you ridden in the pain
of ridiculous regret of days lost and moments
far removed.
Bitterness serves no purpose in this
Leaping life; it does but bury us in a closet
Of coldness, ripping our hearts at the seams 'til
no blood flows; dry, dark; empty.
Let love in, fill your heart with fortune's
forgiveness;
For in letting go of ignorant indifferences
And selfish sways, your heart shall dress
Your soul in love so great, just as the
Glittering reflections of the rainbow's song
Dance in the summer rain;
As the peaceful dove sweeps in,
Unpicking your thorns and evaporating your
pointless pain;
Leaving your floating in freedom's feathers;
Of eternal empathetic love.

❤ **Bitterness does not serve us. Fury does not free us. Grudges engulf our hearts in envy and clouds of grey and pierce us with pain. Let your past go. Try forgive someone you never thought you could forgive. You'll be surprised how much it will set you free. What's the point in holding on to anger, in hating someone because of a past version of themselves. Sometimes in life we like to hold on to** our pain, because it becomes part of who we are. Rewrite the ending of this chapter in your book of life. Changing one chapter could give you the happy ending you've always dreamed of. ♥

Heaven's horizons

Heaven's horizon, hidden in the
Flavorous folds of earth's endless ether;
Pink rays dancing gently on the careful clouds
As they float peacefully yet persistently
Through the aromatic abyss of silent songs
And joyful dances. Beaming blissfully,
The sun smiles radiant rainbows,
Casting her sensuous spell over the
Misty mirage of careful colours;
Emanating magical mixes of purposeful petal pinks,
Brave blues and yearning yellows;
As they blend in loving perfection on the
amorous love-struck horizon.
Nature's simple careful complexity;
A stunning sight for excited eyes
And dancing hearts;
A scene for lover's nights
And dreaming hearts;
A love for broken souls
And shattered spirits;
A healing hand;
A gentle gift;
Luscious life;
Boundless;
Beautiful;
Bliss;
LOVE.

Aiméè Keenan

♥ Have you ever looked out the window of an aeroplane and wondered how on earth you got here? Ever just stared, in awe of the world, wondering how it's just so beautiful? These are the beautiful gifts you get when you choose to awaken. Gratitude. ♥

Unfortunate flames

A beautiful poison,
Trapped in your radiant rays,
Saddened by my unrequited ways,
Mixed up in magic and logic's love;
Torn by your summer smile; sweet as rain on
a spring Sunday morn.
I mourn this sorry scene; everlasting yet
forever gone; dead in thy rushing refusal.
Daydreams dance through my merry mind,
Witnessing a hundred worlds of worriless
wonders,
Cying in critical crotchets and saddened
semibreves over our sordid silent story.
Conflicting chapters of the same blissful book;
Incomplete -
Pages ripped at the seams
By fear's furious fingers;
Stealing away the flame of my tearful twin,
As our unity crawls off into the night
In a cloud of mysterious madness -
Saving the line, the moment; the resolution, for
another play, another book, another world,
Another body: another life.

♥**If you start believing that everything happens for a reason, life becomes a lot more interesting, a lot more peaceful and lot happier.** ♥

Soul's perfection

Nothing shines so bright as those blue eyes
spit glitter in the night; dancing, glowing,
singing.
Nothing holds my heart as your soul does;
Vibrant, radiant, humble; Perfection.

♥**You are imperfectly perfect.** ♥

......You ARE ENOUGH. ♥

TRUST YOUR GUT♥

BELIEVE IN YOU ♥